A to Z

Motivational Affirmations

Sonya Bhalla

Cover design, mandala designs
and written content by:
Sonya Bhalla
ISBN (paperback): 978-9948-754-70-1

Dedication

For anyone who needs some self-love
or self-assuring affirmations to brighten their day
or set them on a path to build a resilient
inner voice and positive mindset.

Introduction

This book contains motivational affirmations for personal goals or attributes from A to Z.

Affirmations are positive statements intended to help you believe in yourself and encourage a positive inner voice and frame of mind. They can instil confidence in your abilities and uplift your spirit and raise your energetic frequency.

You can read this book every day, or as and when needed to give you a boost of empowering words when times get a little tough, or to just help reinforce your core values.

A to Z Motivational Affirmations

A to Z

Motivational Affirmations

Sonya Bhalla

Sonya Bhalla

A is for being

AMBITIOUS

enough to reach
for the stars
and achieve my goals.

Sonya Bhalla

B is for being

BEAUTIFUL

in every way –
mind, body
and soul.

Sonya Bhalla

C is for being

CREATIVE

because
I have great ideas,
inspire others,
and find
problem-solving fun.

Sonya Bhalla

D is for being

DETERMINED

to stay the course,
work hard and
get my jobs done.

Sonya Bhalla

E is for being

EXTRAORDINARY

because I always aim
to go above and beyond.

Sonya Bhalla

F is for being

FRIENDLY

because
I build and value
strong social bonds.

G is for being

GRATEFUL

for everything
and everyone
in my life.

H is for being

HELPFUL

to anyone
who needs comfort,
care or advice.

Sonya Bhalla

I is for being

INDEPENDENT

enough to make
my own choices
and fulfil all my needs.

Sonya Bhalla

J is for being

JUST

and fair in how
I listen, respect
and interact with
everyone I meet.

Sonya Bhalla

K is for being

KNOWLEDGEABLE

as I love to learn
new things
and discover the
world around me.

Sonya Bhalla

L is for being

LOGICAL

in my approach
to review, consider and reason before
I react, believe or agree.

Sonya Bhalla

M is for being

MINDFUL

of my words and actions,
especially how they can
affect other people.

Sonya Bhalla

N is for being

NEAT

because organising
everything in the right place
allows easier retrieval.

Sonya Bhalla

O is for

OPTIMISTIC

as I radiate happy vibes
and have a positive
mindset and attitude.

Sonya Bhalla

P is for being

PROUD

of who I am,
my achievements
and ability to
embrace new opportunities
with gratitude.

Sonya Bhalla

Q is for being

QUICK

at grasping
new concepts,
and efficiently managing
my workloads.

Sonya Bhalla

R is for being

RESILIENT

because I never
give-up.
I overcome problems
with strength and resolve,
so I can learn and grow.

Sonya Bhalla

S is for being

SENSIBLE

with my decisions,
and knowing when
to ask for help
and when to say no.

Sonya Bhalla

T is for being

TRUSTWORTHY

so others can confidently rely on
everything
I say, do and know.

Sonya Bhalla

U is for being

UNIQUE

because I'm special,
yet humble and strive to be
the best version of myself.

Sonya Bhalla

V is for being

VOCAL

about my thoughts,
feelings and rights to protect my
physical and mental health.

Sonya Bhalla

W is for being

WORTHY

of self-love,
self-respect,
self-care and compassion
when I have
problems to solve.

Sonya Bhalla

X is for

XENACIOUS

as I adapt to change with ease
because I believe in
self-development to improve and
evolve.

Sonya Bhalla

Y is for

YOUTHFUL

by being full of energy,
being honest, modest
and healthy in every way.

Sonya Bhalla

Z is for having a

ZESTFUL

personality with a happy, and content
outlook to life,
today, and always.

About the author

Sonya lives in Dubai with her family and is the mother of three wonderful children. Her favourite pastime is to write whenever time permits. She loves writing poetry and writing for children, so look out for her other books. She also loves the cinema, watching documentaries, reading, travelling, and spending time with family and friends.

For more of her inspired writing, and to see her positive poetry posters, follow her Instagram page @positive.poetry.posters

This book is published by Sonya Bhalla under the Published Printing & Text Permit issued by the Ministry of Culture and Youth (MCY) under number MC-01-01-5546778. The age group to which the content of the book is appropriate according to the age classification system issued by the Emirates Media Council is E.